From the Streets to Real Happiness & Peace

Elizabeth Ash

Copyright ©2018, Elizabeth Ash

All rights reserved. No part of this publication may be reproduced, distributed, or transmitted in any form or by any means, including photocopying, scanning, recording, or other electronic or mechanical methods, without the prior written permission of the author, except in the case of brief quotations embodied in critical reviews and certain other noncommercial uses permitted by copyright law.

Distribution of this e-book without the prior permission of the author is illegal, and therefore punishable by law. It is not legal to reproduce, duplicate or transmit any part of this document either in printed format or electronically. It is strictly prohibited to record this publication and storage of the document is not allowed without written permission from the author. All rights reserved.

Disclaimer

Legal Notice: - Elizabeth Ash and the accompanying materials have used their best efforts in preparing the material. This book has been composed with the best intention of providing correct and reliable information. The information provided is offered solely for informational purposes and is universal as so. This information is presented without contract or any type of guarantee assurance.

Elizabeth Ash makes no representation or warranties with respect to the accuracy, applicability, fitness or completeness of the contents of this book. The information contained in this book is strictly for educational purposes. Therefore, if you wish to apply ideas contained in this book, you are taking full responsibility for your actions.

Elizabeth Ash disclaims any warranties (express or implied), merchantability, or fitness for any particular purpose. Elizabeth Ash shall in no event be held liable to any party for any direct, indirect, punitive, special, incidental or other consequential damages arising directly or indirectly from any use of this material, which is provided "as is", and without warranties.

Any and all trademarks used in this book are owned by the owners themselves, are not affiliated with this book and for clarifying purposes only.

As always, the advice of a competent medical, legal, tax, accounting or other professional should be sought. Elizabeth Ash does not warrant the performance, effectiveness or applicability of any sites listed or linked to in this book. All links are for information purposes only and are not warranted for content, accuracy or any other implied or explicit purpose.

This book is not intended as a substitute for the medical advice of physicians. The reader should regularly consult a physician in matters relating to his/her health and particularly with respect to any symptoms that may require diagnosis or medical attention.

ISBN: 978-1-7324365-6-5

To all those out there still searching for hope...

Contents

Chapter 1: The Point Of No Return........ 9

Chapter 2: My Backstory...................... 17

Chapter 3: The Cold Night Of Change.. 21

Chapter 4: My Brother's Keeper 31

Chapter 5: The Final Moment 39

Chapter 6: A Grain of Hope................. 41

Chapter 7: The Test 46

Chapter 8: Proof................................... 50

Chapter 9: One Thing.......................... 52

Stay In Touch 55

Chapter 1:
The Point Of No Return

They say once you've experienced your own personal hell, you'll know.

Well, they're right. And you never forget.

****

He was a monster attacking his prey.

Rushing at me, he pinned my young body between the metal wall of his converted bus and his huge burly frame, his true misogynistic nature raw and unexposed. His two hands affixed themselves to the sides of my soft thin neck as he threw back his head in a spin-chilling laugh of derision. I struggled as best as I could, but my attempts to escape only seemed to egg him on.

This was a game, his game… and I had no idea how to play. He had suddenly transformed from the gentle guy I'd met at the street corner into a deranged psychopath.

"Please, Jimmy, please," I begged, the tears streaming down the side of my face.

The more I kicked and scratched, the more he fixated on my neck, his odious flesh pressing harder against me. No matter how hard I hit him, he never flinched or even budged. It was as if he felt no pain at all.

"You thought you could just blow me and get away with a thousand dollars that easily?" He was laughing at me with a wild kind of crazy that bordered on horror picture lunacy.

He'd looked like such a dummy when I first saw him. How could I have been such a poor judge of character?

But the life of a hooker isn't easy. And most of the sordid tales you hear are true.

Sometimes you're out working the parks or hanging out by the bars. Sometimes it's a street corner where you knew the guys went looking for action.

I'd usually get someone every day and have something to take home at the end of the night. It wasn't much, but it was enough to keep the wolf away from the door.

And every once-in-awhile, I'd find a guy with real money. Or one just too stupid or out of it to know what was going on. That's who I thought this guy was. Some loser stoned on drugs and half drunk. And now the price of my poor judgement was being paid in spades.

Jimmy was neither.

He was a thoroughly nauseating human, living a life made up of various shades of miserable. Scruffy oily hair, a protruding belly, bad breath from the drinking and a disgusting body odor that came from God knows where. This guy obviously fulfilled his libido episodes only with hookers. I mean, who would date this guy?

He'd approached me in a half-sauntered walk, portraying his lack of control from the high he was on.

"How much for the night?" His voice was raspy and deep in a low guttural sort of way.

This was not my kind of john. I quoted him so high I figured he'd scoff and walk away.

"$1000." I looked him right in the eye with a smirk of derision on my face. I was so much better than this miserable creature, even if I was a hooker.

To my utter surprise and simultaneous dismay, he took the deal. "Cool, let's go. I'll pay you in the cab." He hailed one down and I got in, thinking I'd hit easy street for once.

I couldn't believe my luck. I mean, who wouldn't take a deal like that. This would make up for all the slow nights and give me some breathing room. Plus, I figured he was so far gone I'd be out of there with a quick blow job and home free for the night. Maybe he was such a schmuck I'd end up being his personal hooker and could work him forever.

I had no idea I was about to take on a demon in men's clothing. This Jimmy, or whoever he was, had become my biggest mistake.

"Stop struggling, bitch! I'll teach you!"

He swung his head backward and slammed me hard in the forehead. He meant business.

The pain was overwhelming. Then it all went black. When I opened my eyes, it was an entirely different story.

****

His rough dirty hands were now caressing the side of my cheek. "Hello angel. Is daddy's little girl awake now?"

His voice had a deep condescending coo to it. And his menacing eyes mocked me with every word.

"So pretty. Thinking you're so much better than dirty old Jimmy. With your deep brown eyes and long wavy hair, all sexy and dolled up. Don't feel quite so superior now, do you? But I can make you just as dirty as me."

He moved in close and started licking my face, his saliva thick and sticky, accompanied by the rotten egg stench of his breath.

"Now little angel, don't say a word." An evil smile seemed to be glued to his face. "Just relax and enjoy tonight. Enjoy everything."

Get the hell out of this bed and run! I thought to myself. But when I tried to move I realized that was impossible. I couldn't move anything. Not my hands or my legs. Nothing.

I finally started to get my bearings and the full impact of where I was came at me.

I was tied fast with zip ties firmly binding me to the walls and ends of the bed… spread-eagle and completely helpless. He could do anything he wanted.

"I know you want this too, so just be calm. Struggling won't get you anywhere. Besides, you don't want to miss what I have planned for you."

He pointed to a small free-standing tray he'd placed beside the bed. I gasped! Oh, dear God! There was a whip, a mound of cocaine and long wooden peg with a deep groove running down its entire length.

Scared doesn't even begin to describe what I was feeling.

Please let this be a bad dream. Please, dear God, let me wake up from this nightmare!

"Don't cry, angel, don't cry." He almost seemed to pity me at that point. Maybe that could be my way out of this horror.

"Please, don't hurt me," I begged, tears rolling down my face. "What is it you want from me?"

I couldn't control the trembling in my voice. He knew I was frightened, and somehow that just made him more tenacious.

"You want to know, angel? Well, then, dirty Jimmy will tell you. I'm going to whip you and watch you bleed and cry. And right when you think you can't take any more, I'm going to shove that long grooved peg inside your hole and fill your insides with that mound of cocaine. I'll watch your eyes roll back in your head and your body convulse in seizures. And when that happens, I'll know I got my $1000 worth."

I knew at that moment this man was probably going to kill me, painfully and slowly. I couldn't stop shaking and crying and every word from my mouth became an uttered plea for mercy. All hope was lost, and I knew it.

Then I heard it!

The loud banging knock on the door of Jimmy's converted old bus. It reverberated through the metal frame of the bus, getting louder and louder.

"Open up, Jimmy!" A deep baritone voice of authority barreled through the air.

Jimmy froze, his narrow eyes now bulging to twice their size. For the first time that night, he was scared.

"Shhhh… don't say a word," he whispered softly, covering my mouth with his hand.

This was it. My only chance. Out of pure instinct I bit his finger as hard as I could, his filthy blood flowing into my mouth from the voracity of the bite.

He screamed in pain, pulling the bloodied hand back in shock at my audacity. And I screamed even louder to whoever was there in hopes they would hear me.

"Help me! Help!"

Could it be? Finally, a glimmer of hope?

Chapter 2:
My Backstory

At this point, you're probably wondering how I ever got myself into such a lifestyle to begin with. While my story isn't unique, it's true. And hopefully by learning what happened to me, you'll be able to help yourself or someone else avoid the mistakes I made. Because that is the reason I'm writing this story.

My situation had led me to a point in life where... I felt... the only thing I had to sell was me.

My father died when I was eight years old. That left my mother and four kids, of which I was the oldest. Mom spent the next six years working three jobs trying to keep food on the table and some semblance of a roof over our heads.

But despite all her hard work, we still ended up in a deplorable two room apartment in the slums of New York City. Since mom had no work skills to offer an employer, the jobs she got were menial, but they were honest. And this was the best she could do.

I know it must've been one of the most difficult times in her life. I watched as a woman who always had a warm smile that melted everyone's heart, suddenly become brooding and bitter.

At first, I didn't understand why she changed toward us, always nagging and yelling. I thought dad's death was just too much for her and she was consumed by grief. It wasn't until later that I discovered that wasn't it at all. It was the responsibility of having to raise four kids with no skills, education or help from anyone.

After six years of nearly working herself to death, she started to get weaker and forgetful. Sometimes she'd stutter or just zone out for awhile. The more she worked, the worse it got. And the worse it got, the less she was able to work. Until finally, she got fired from all her jobs because she just couldn't focus and think long enough to complete anything.

And without any money for doctors, there was no way for her to get help. If we'd known she had a brain tumor, they'd have taken it out right away and things would've gotten better so much faster. But that didn't happen and we had no money then to find out.

It was tough without my dad, but it was never as tough as when mom couldn't work anymore. At the young age of 14, I was faced with the hard reality of life as the first child. I needed to do something. I needed to fend for my family.

Hot tears flow from my eyes as I write this part. Even though years have passed now, the memories of what I felt compelled to do for family survival seem unthinkable.

After all, I was still just a child. It shouldn't have been me. There should've been some kind of assistance from somewhere. But there wasn't. And I wouldn't wish those heart rending experiences on my worst enemy.

My first instinct was to support my family, even if it meant begging in the streets. And this was where the majority of my nightmares began.

I have a lot of stories to share about how I lived my life. I struggled through unimaginable things.

But the truth I came to discover is this. We are the authors of our own life script. Regardless of whatever life throws at you, you are ultimately above them and you can decide the course of your life.

In retrospect, I can only be grateful for the strength I had to get through it all. That strength gave me the courage to become the new me that is able to teach others how to live above their nightmares.

If there's any point I want to emphasize in this book, it's that your change begins with you. It starts from the incorrigible disgust for the kind of life you're currently living.

I conquered the streets, but it wasn't easy. And now you need to know how it began.

Chapter 3:
The Cold Night Of Change

It all started on a cold winter night.

I pressed my forehead against the window of our small shabby apartment and watched as Mom crossed the street into our four-story brownstone. The color on her face was completely drained and she looked almost ghost-like. Each gawky stride she took seemed to tax what little strength she had left.

Apart from her long ungainly legs that looked like noodles, the way she kept stopping as she walked toward our dilapidated building told me something was wrong. Little did I know the thoughts that would transpire in my mind that night. Thoughts that would forever change the shape of our lives.

Finally, her figure creeped out of sight as she headed into the front door.

Mom opened the front door and darted over to the radiator trying to warm herself. Her glove-veiled hands were dipped deep into the pockets of the tattered winter coat. Shivering, she hovered over the radiator in an effort to erase the bone-chilling cold from her body.

Mom didn't seem to notice any of us. Not fevered Samantha wrapped in an old thick quilt or Amy playing with her headless doll; or Tyler, who's never-filled-tummy constantly cried out of emptiness.

Tyler was always hungry. Often, he'd sneak out of the house in search of something to eat. He'd become a regular at some of the restaurants, constantly begging for food. If he got enough, he'd bring it back for us, but that didn't always happen.

"How does she feel now?" Mom's voice was weak and distant but the concern for her youngest was still there. She moved closer to where Samantha lay and began to wipe the sweat off her little face.

It was sad seeing my mother watch her youngest child fevered and trembling. There used to be a free clinic, but it got shut down due to a lack of funding. So, the whole neighborhood was without any real medical attention or anyone who even remotely cared what happened to us.

Of course, mom tried to help Samantha, but her own health issues were getting worse. She'd be alright for awhile, then all of a sudden, she'd get confused and couldn't keep track of where she was or what she was doing. She always seemed to get by long enough to land a part time job. And she'd get through just enough days to bring home a little money. But the rent was always late. And there was never enough to put any more than the scarcest meal on the table.

"She's nothing close to being better, mom." I stroked Samantha's hot flushed cheek as I continued talking.

"I wasn't able to get anything for her at the pharmacy. They insisted I pay our bill in full before giving us anything else."

I sighed. I could feel the desperation inside me as I looked at my sister just laying there, not knowing what was happening to her.

"I'm sorry. I'm sorry for not…" Then mom broke down beside Samantha, the tears staining her face and falling onto her faded yellow collar. I could see the pain in mom's face as she struggled with her own illness and the effects of it huddled inside the old dirty quilt.

As I looked at her that night, I knew I had to do something. I knew my mom wasn't capable any more. If one of us didn't do something, we'd all be split apart, and mom would be locked away God knows where. It was at that moment that I knew. It could only be me… only me.

"It's going to be fine mother," I whispered softly as I brushed the fallen brown hair back behind her ear.

Even though I knew those words were not so much a promise but a soothing phrase to calm her, I still believed them. I believed it would all change one day… somehow. Though that seemed like the second coming of Christ at that moment.

Nevertheless, I knew what to do; or so I thought. I'd made a decision in my mind and couldn't see past it.

In my mind the survival of the family depended on me. I was determined to pull us out of this misery.

There was a price to pay for my naivety. A price I was soon to discover.

Later that night, I walked down the street mulling the scene over and over in my head. I was completely buried in my own thoughts when a car honked and pulled over. Somewhat agitated, I watched the window of the vintage car roll down. I knew who it was. The one person in the neighborhood I had always tried to avoid… it was Leo.

Leo was the leader of one of the neighborhood gangs. Everyone knew him or of him, and he reveled in the notoriety. He had a record that included drug dealing, assault, and alleged connections to murder, but that could never be proven.

He'd followed me home from school, more than once. Always calling out, making big promises. Leo loved a challenge. And that's all he ever got from me.

Mom warned me about him every time she heard his name. "He's crazy and he's no good. You stay away from the likes of him, Lizzy."

But that night was different; it was completely different. I was a lost soul wandering the street looking for help anywhere I could find it. I wasn't going against mother's warnings just to rebel. I only wanted to save my family.

When Leo finally got out of the car, he pulled the cigarette from his mouth and exhaled slowly, acting as cocky as he always did.

"Where you goin' this late? Maybe I can give you a ride."

That night his voice sounded like that of a guardian angel rather than a subtle devil. He walked toward me and the fear started to kick in. I should've paid attention to that fear, that inner warning built into me.

"I'm not gonna hurt you. Look. All you have to do is spend one night with me and your money problems will be over."

I was scared of losing my virginity to him, but my reason for staying glued to the spot won over. I remembered my mom I'd left crying at home. Tyler's constant whining he was hungry. And Samantha who couldn't get the medicine she needed.

I knew exactly what I was doing; at least that's what I told myself. At that moment, right and wrong meant nothing. And family meant everything.

I know what you're thinking. There's always another way, another choice. I could get a job. Really? Doing what? And even if someone would hire me, I was 14. How much money could someone my age hope to make at minimum wage with limited hours.

"How much would I get for a night?" That moment I lifted my face and watched his. I was staring into the eyes of the man who was going to turn me from a girl into a woman.

Leo was stunned. That was not what he expected.

"I said, how much will you give for a night?"

The sound of those words grew into abomination as they rattled through my brain.

I repeated them once more and he chortled. He looked at me and knew something had changed. The shy young girl who'd always resisted him was gone. He couldn't find her anymore.

"What does $500 sound like?"

He looked me square in the eye, a sneering smile lifting the corner of his mouth.

He knew I could never reject the offer, let alone negotiate a better one. He knew all about me. He knew my mother was getting worse and couldn't keep a job, and that we barely had enough to eat. And he knew I must be completely desperate to let him get this close to me. I was ripe for the plucking, and he loved it.

"What if I threw in dinner? I bet you're hungry."

His words actually made me feel worse, like an animal he was about to feed then sell to the highest bidder. Nevertheless, my need for money had already won out. And I hadn't eaten all day.

With resolute assignation, I turned and walked over to the passenger door and got in.

Leo just stood there watching in amazement. For him it was a night come true. He didn't say a word. Just jumped into the driver's seat and started up the engine.

****

True to his word, we'd eaten at one of the nicer Italian restaurants in the neighborhood. But that didn't stall the inevitable very long.

Before I knew it, we were at his place. He placed his hand around my waist and firmly escorted me to the front door.

Something kept gnawing at the back of my mind… *there has to be a better way.* But that little voice didn't stand a chance against the pressing reality of a sick starving family.

Leo ushered me straight into the bedroom, not bothering to put on the lights. Immediately, he pushed me down onto his bed and rushed at me like a predator feasting on its prey. He locked lips with me and rocked his cigarette stained tongue in and out of my mouth. It was a disgusting experience. And it was, in fact, the first time I had been kissed like that. Leo got what he'd always wanted that night. And I got my first taste of depravity.

After long hours of painful sex with me, Leo dropped me at the south end of my block and paid me off. As I got out of the car, a sinking feeling of what I'd done began to churn in my stomach. I could still feel his stench all over me; his sweat and saliva still staining my skin, and the hurt between my legs still throbbing.

"Thanks for increasing my pain," I quipped as I walked away. I was sure he would never understand those words. Even if he did, they would probably mean nothing to him. Just like he meant nothing to me.

Most mistakes are done out of ignorance or even sheer stupidity. That night, mine was not. It was, in fact, a conscious act. One I'd committed out of pity and love. Whether I now view it as right or wrong is completely irrelevant. It was an act of survival.

I didn't care what anyone thought about me at that point. They couldn't possibly make me feel any dirtier than I already did. But before you judge me too harshly, let me go on with my story.

The short walk down the block to our little apartment took almost forever. I felt different and weak. And I was trying to make my arrival home as discreet as possible. I felt so obvious; I was sure it must've shown.

Walking down the dimly lit hallway to our front door, I gently grasped the door knob and twisted it slowly.

The door opened silently, but the old wooden floor creaked my presence as I walked in.

As I turned from the door, mother's eyes greeted me, her arms crossed tightly across her chest.

"You don't have to hide anything." There was no anger in her voice. Just a touch of sadness.

I glanced at her, afraid to meet her gaze for more than a moment. The room was almost dark, with only a small night light glowing in the corner, causing ominous shadows to flee across the room.

I looked down at the floor and walked away to my little spot in the bedroom all of us kids shared.

"Goodnight mama," was all I could get out.

I knew she wanted me to explain where I'd been and why I came home so late. But I had the feeling she already knew.

Exactly what I'd done and why was more than I could share that night. It was a secret I had to keep.

Chapter 4:
My Brother's Keeper

The money from Leo went quickly. No one really questioned where it came from too much. If anyone said anything, I lied and said I'd gotten a part-time delivery job for the deli and they paid me cash under the table. I know mom didn't really believe it, but her ability to keep track of what was going on around her wasn't getting any better, and most of the time she faded away into her own oblivious world.

Our needs continued to grow. There was never enough to eat, and mom's condition would come and go. Sometimes she struggled with our names and repeated things she'd said just five minutes before. Then there were the times when she seemed mostly normal, just distant and unattached.

As for me, I believed life was just unfair. And it seemed the more I believed it, the worse things got. But at least I had a way to bring in money now. I was able to hold things together, but just barely. I never thought about how much longer I could pull it off. Just that we were getting by today.

You can imagine the trauma of accidentally becoming the head of the family at my age. The stress of having everyone look to you for answers, food, protection. I had become the mother hen whose chicks sought shelter under wings. Except my wings were barely there, I was so young.

Then one night Tyler went out and didn't come back. At first, I thought he'd decided to stay with Joey, his best friend. And like anyone would do, I went to check on him the next day.

Tyler was different from Samantha and Amy, the two youngest. Their world was at home, still unaware of what was happening around them.

But Tyler was second oldest. Even though he was a young boy at best, he believed he should be free. Free to go anywhere at any time and mingle with whoever he chose.

He never cared about how small he was or the fact that he still couldn't fend for himself. He saw life simplistically and felt the problems of the streets had nothing to do with him.

Joey was just a couple of blocks over, so it was easy to swing by and check up on him. But when I got there, Tyler wasn't. And Joey was scared.

"Tyler has been taken by Leo's men," he cried. "I got him into this. I'm so sorry."

"Wait… Leo's men?"

I began to rack my head for what he could've done or perhaps what they did. For all I knew, Leo was never so crazy he would kidnap my brother for no reason. I was sure they must've done something terrible.

I held Joey by the shoulders to try to calm him down. "What did you do, Joey?"

He broke down completely and buried his head on my shoulder. And just like the kid he was, he made me promise not to get angry or tell anyone about it.

Finally, he regained his composure enough to tell me what happened. "We stole from him."

His voice was quiet as he said those words and he couldn't look me in the eye. He knew he was in big trouble and that Tyler was in even worse.

But those four words were enough. They were enough for me to imagine the situation Tyler was in. And it was enough to know that Leo would be waiting for me to come and bail him out.

"He said he needed money to take care of his sick mother and sister," Joey continued.

Wow, I thought to myself, wondering how he'd managed to conceal his love for us. I'd always thought he was off in his own world and didn't feel a part of us, but I was wrong.

That was all I needed to hear. I left Joey's house dead set on a mission to get my little brother back. And I knew exactly where to go.

I ran as fast as my legs could take me, darting around people on the sidewalks, trying not to get hit running across the streets. It wasn't far now. Leo's place was just a few yards away.

Breathless, I went to his front door and pounded as hard as I could. The adrenaline was pumping, and even though I'd run quite a distance, I still had a good head of steam.

When Leo answered the door he was completely nonplussed, his demeanor even more arrogant than usual. He knew he was in control.

"I guess you heard what your brother did. But I doubt you understand the gravity, so let me clue you in."

He took a drag on his cigarette, expelled the smoke through his nose to show off a bit and continued.

"Your brother, or as I call him, 'the little thief,' stole a bag of money meant for a business deal. Now, the issue is not the money, but the time wasted."

He stopped yet again, caressing a half-naked girl beside him in the doorway.

"My business partner is ranting at the moment and I don't have the time to explain things to him. So, this is what you're going to do. You'll take the stolen money and give it to him. And when I know you've kept up your end, I'll give you back your brother."

"Alive...", I emphasized.

"Yes, alive."

There was a bad omen that hung in the air. Somehow, I knew there was more to this. I just didn't know what. And I couldn't even imagine what was about to come.

Leo turned and made a call to his business partner.

Pay for it? Did I hear that right? I didn't hear it all, but somehow, he made it sound like I was the cause of the problem and was ready to pay for the time wasted.

That question kept popping up in my head over and over. I knew I was a fool to have thought things could be that simple. And even though my mind was screaming *NO!* to the deal, the need to save Tyler was all I could comprehend.

****

I was scared out of my mind. I knew something was wrong somewhere. I just didn't know what.

Why didn't Leo want to go or send any of his men? Why was he so interested in waiting for me to show up to fix the blown deal?

Those were the questions that flew around in my head as I walked toward three husky men standing beside a black Mercedes. None of them looked like they understood much English, but I didn't care. My only interest was in saving my brother and getting us back home alive.

With as much bravery as I could muster, I walked closer to them and stopped. Two of them moved toward me. But as soon as the guy in the car opened his door, they immediately halted.

I'd never seen anyone quite like him before. He had a wounded eye covered up with a black patch, like a pirate, with a wad of chewing tobacco protruding in his left cheek. He was definitely the head man. This was the guy Leo called his business partner.

A chilling sensation of dread ran down my spine. I was in so much panic, I stood frozen to the spot. I wanted to turn and run but nothing in my body would respond.

The one-eyed man walked up to me, his demeanor powerful, but silent. Without saying a word, he belted me on the side of the head and knocked me to the ground. Then two of his thugs grabbed me and dragged me bleeding back to their car.

They drove me to an old warehouse where they had a make-shift office with an old mattress on the floor. Still half dazed from the knock on the head and pounding pain, they ripped my clothes off and started in on me. One by one, they raped every hole in my body. I was like a rag doll trapped in a surreal painting of terror that had come to life. At some point I must've passed out completely, but I doubt if that stopped them.

All I could remember was them passing me around until everyone got their turn. Then they shoved me back in the car and dumped me at Leo's. The head guy made it clear they'd kill me if I breathed a word, but not after watching them brutalize my family first, the way they'd just done to me.

Leo opened his front door and just stood there looking at me, still lying on the ground where they'd left me, bleeding and barely conscious.

"He did this to you, not me. You better get in here and get yourself cleaned up."

That night, he had Tyler brought to his apartment. Then he released us and threw cash at us as he shut the door laughing. I wanted to throw it right back at him, but the rent was due, and we desperately needed food and medicine.

As we walked home in shame, I began to think about a lot of things. If Leo would pay me that much for the way his business partner had treated me, what would lust-filled men who thought I was beautiful pay me?

I knew the hooker life was never what I wanted for myself, but the little voice in my head was completely drowned out at this point.

That night changed my entire world. My view toward life, my body and my self-worth… if there was any of that left at all. I was just an empty shell. And I had no idea how to fill it up again.

And now you know how I came to be a hooker. And what led me to the point we started with at the beginning of this story, almost two years later. I'll finish it up for you now.

Chapter 5:
The Final Moment

The knock on the door of Jimmy's old converted bus had now become a frenzied pounding.

That, added to the pain Jimmy was now feeling from the chunk of flesh I'd just bitten out of his finger, threw him off his guard.

Then I heard a loud crash as the stranger at the door kicked it open.

There was a commanding voice, deep and masculine. I turned my head as best I could to see what was going on, but my view was partially blocked by an interior hall wall. Whoever he was, he was my savior. And at that point, I didn't care whose side of the law he was on.

By now Jimmy had started to regain his composure and came at me with pure rage in his eyes. He gripped my neck as hard as he could and started squeezing with all the strength his added fury now gave him. I screamed with what little breath I could get out, but it wasn't much.

My eardrums almost shattered from what I heard next. A loud blast that ricocheted through the bus serving as Jimmy's domicile.

One thing I knew. If you hear the sound of a gunshot, then the bullet must've missed you or you've been hit and you're still alive. That night I heard three shots.

Jimmy's grip around my neck weakened and he crashed beside the bed. He was dead. It took a moment for all that to register with me. I was sobbing hysterically, gasping to get the air back into my lungs.

It was a cop who'd come to save me that day. He was there exactly when I needed him.

He threw a cover over my naked body and began releasing me from the ties.

By this time, back-up and an ambulance had arrived. There was a barrage of questions, flashing lights and strangers pouring over every inch of the scene.

I was in shock and it all seemed like a blur. The ambulance ride, the hospital, the police statements. All of it. A terrible collage made up of the worst moments of my life.

Chapter 6:
A Grain of Hope

I couldn't seem to forget my encounter with Jimmy… the pain and how I nearly died. It was as though it just happened, and that it never happened, at the same time.

For the next week, I stayed in the small shared bedroom. Mother came knocking on the door, but I never answered. For the first three days she left me alone, thinking I would come out and talk when I was ready. But I wasn't.

In the meantime, she let Tyler, Amy and Samantha pass the nights with her on their make-shift cots in the living room.

There were days when she would kneel beside my bed, begging me to eat and take a bath, but I was never interested. My bed and pillow remained my closest friends. They dried my tears, held me in the middle of the night, and kept me warm when the terror of my personal hell replayed itself in my dreams.

All I wanted to do was keep to myself. Mother worried, but it really didn't register with me. It was as though I was battling a demon inside me. My days were dedicated to a constant drifting in and out of an endless fog and my nights were a reflection of my days. I was only half alive.

Soon, I realized I couldn't fight this alone. I couldn't break free by myself. I knew there was a need to talk, to let someone in. I gave in to the only person who stood with me when father died. The only person who would never complain she was carrying too many crosses on her shoulder. I gave in to my mother.

That night lasted almost forever. For the first thirty minutes we didn't speak. She just held my hand and let me cry. She looked thinner than ever. But, thankfully, she seemed to have her wits about her that night.

Then I had the courage to look into her eyes. For the first time since my father died, I saw her cry. The more I looked, the more I saw the pain hoarded up there for years. The pain we never knew about. She seemed in much worse shape than I.

It was more than I could take, and I looked away. Away from her wet grey eyes and pale tear stained cheeks. But I could still feel her hands trembling as she held mine.

Even while I was looking away, my soul felt a connection I thought I'd lost when dad died. I felt at peace with her. Somehow, I knew she understood.

She sat down on the bed and held me like a mother holds a long-lost child. This was what I needed. My mother's touch and love.

I hugged her back, as long and hard as I could. I knew then it would all be okay. That terrible night I'd endured on that rickety bus would somehow be a new beginning.

She softly touched my cheek and spoke. "Don't let it stay this way. You can break free. You can be anything. Don't let these just be words. Let them become your power."

Her words were soft and strangely piercing. I'd never heard my mother talk like that before. It was as if an angel was speaking through her voice.

Then she kissed me on the forehead and told me to rest, turning out the light when she left.

Those words were like a life raft thrown to a drowning man at sea.

She set off hope and dreams in me. And those few words woke something up in my soul and gave that little voice a stage again.

I could break free. I could be who I wanted to be. She showed me a way to get past the fear. She showed me I had the power within myself to change me.

Suddenly I felt relief. I laughed and cried at the same time. A joy I'd never felt swept over me as I said the words again and again.

I can break free. I can be anything. I can change me.

The more I said the words the more relief I felt. I just kept repeating them over and over until they became a song in my head, lifting me higher and higher out my depression.

I can break free. I can be anything. I can change me.

All those old nagging thoughts of how or when didn't even matter anymore. All that mattered was the feeling of change happening inside me at that moment. And that change would somehow bring me the how and when.

The next morning, I woke up and felt happy for the first time in years. And there were those words again, shaping my world the moment I opened my eyes.

I could do it. I could get past my pain and desperation. I could put myself back on track. But this time, with possibilities I would allow to come and not turn away.

Somehow, I knew if I kept saying the words and feeling the feelings, things would get better. Yes, I know that sounds overly simplistic and unrealistic, but it worked. Not a huge miracle in one day. But slowly and with a grain of hope I never had before, my life began to change.

I just kept thinking it, saying it, feeling it. The more I focused on the words and how it made me feel, the stronger I got, and the more life started to turn around.

Chapter 7:
The Test

We'd been living off the savings I'd made as a hooker, but those monies wouldn't last forever. And mom was somehow getting better and able to work part-time again, so that was helping, too.

I knew it was time to get back into life. I wanted to get a job. A real job.

Many of you are wondering what makes a high-school dropout turned hooker think she can get anywhere in life. Yet, the trust and belief that was growing in me, proved otherwise.

I started saying the words, but I changed them a little bit this time.

I can break free. I can be anything. I can get a real job.

I said those words to myself over and over. And I didn't just say them, I felt them. And when I said them, happiness would creep in and I'd feel myself smiling. They had become more than words. They'd become a power.

Sometimes Samantha and Amy would catch me almost singing those words to myself and laugh. But then they'd start doing it too. It was contagious. The mood in the whole house lifted. Everyone was smiling again. It was almost a miracle.

A few days later one of our neighbors was talking and said she'd seen a sign down at the deli. They were looking for help. I didn't even stop to ask what kind of help. And the fact it would be the bottom of the pay scale didn't even enter my mind.

I cleaned myself up and headed straight there, chanting my mantra over and over in my head.

I can break free. I can be anything. I can get a real job.

Two days later I got a phone call. It was the deli. They wanted me back for a second interview. Me... a high-school dropout. They wanted to talk to me again. I was ecstatic!

By the time I got back home, everyone was dying to know what happened.

"Well...," I drew the moment out to be a little dramatic. "I got the job! I'll be starting on Monday. It's only part time at minimum wage, but it's a job. A real job!"

That next Monday I made sure I looked as neat as possible and headed to work.

I have to say, I loved it. I poured my heart and soul into everything I did. Whether it was sweeping the floor or waiting on customers or stocking shelves didn't matter. I was determined to be the best I could be.

Soon, the other employees were starting to change, too. They complained less and started helping each other out more. And the customers noticed it. They would often remark how cheery the place seemed to have gotten.

Needless to say, David, the owner, was pleased. Sometimes he'd look at me and ask if I was from planet Earth. Other times, intentionally, he'd leave cash laying around in his office and ask me to go in there and clean. But I wouldn't even touch it. I was committed to being the most honest person there.

But, things don't always go the way you plan. And my turn to trust and believe things end up for the best came around.

David felt someone was stealing from the store. And being the new person, I was the prime suspect. So, I got laid off after just three weeks. Since I knew I wasn't the thief, I knew the truth would eventually come out. But I never stopped using the words. I never stopped believing and feeling.

Chapter 8: Proof

Just because I got fired was no reason to sit around home and feel sorry for myself. I decided to use the time to help myself and my family.

Since we couldn't afford a computer and the Internet (no smart phones then), I started going to the library to catch up on my lost education and look for another job.

Tyler had managed to pick up a paper route. The money he was bringing in helped to put food on the table, plus it kept him busy. He actually liked it. So, I decided to use part of my extra time helping him out. I'd get up early and go along with him. It was good for us. We had fun and got to know each other better than we ever had.

And always the words were ringing in my head.

I can change anything. I can break free.

The words weren't always the same. I'd change them around for whatever I needed at the time. But the more I molded and felt them, the more they molded me.

Exactly two weeks after I'd been fired, my old boss appeared at my door.

He said he was sorry for firing me without any real proof. Turns out it was his son that was stealing.

David said he loved my spirit and how I didn't complain when something unexpected had to be done. And if I would come back to work, he'd give me an increase in pay to make up for his mistake.

You have no idea how much that meant to me. My trust in myself had now become someone else's trust and faith in me.

Then he put the icing on the cake. If I promised to get my GED or go back and finish high school, there would be a management position for me at the store. David also said a friend of his was a tutor, and he'd pay for his services if I would stick to the commitment.

I was shocked! It felt like a dream come true.

At that moment I knew as long as I stayed true to my words, that life would stay true to me.

Chapter 9:
One Thing

If you only take one thing from my story, take this.

The life we live is not orchestrated by an external body or unknown force. It just isn't!

We have the power to influence what life gives us by the choices we make. And those choices are influenced by the words in our head and how they make us feel. We can let those same old thoughts rule us, or we can consciously choose new words that take us to better feelings and a better life.

And don't worry… even if you don't feel the words at first, it doesn't matter. Just keep the new words going. The feeling will come. And with it will come the change you so desperately seek.

It isn't complicated, but it does take diligence… a persistence on your part to pull out of the misery that brought you here today.

But the more you do it, the more things change. And before you know it, life has turned around.

No, you won't know exactly how things are going to happen.

And no, there is no script or perfect plan for everyone to follow. Because you're going to be that plan every moment of every day. Which means you get to be a part of each and every one of those better moments when they happen.

Understand this one thing.

There are no rules. Not one.

We are the ones that create the rules for our own lives with our choices. Whatever step we take is because of the thoughts running in our head and how those thoughts make us feel. Just go back to the words: *I can break free. I can be anything. I can change me.*

Know you have everything it takes to raise above the life you're in right now. You have your choices, your words and your feelings. And that can be a powerful combination if you let it.

Be sure you get this. Let it sink in. And you can start things over right now.

Let the words be your template. And when the opportunities come… and they will… make the choices you know will put joy in your heart.

So, start right now. Louder and louder in your soul until it comes to pass.

I can break free. I can be anything. I can change me.

Never forget…

ONLY YOU CAN CHANGE YOU

Stay In Touch

Thank you for reading my story. I hope it helps at least one person take the first step upward out of their personal abyss. If that person is you, then I am honored you heard my words.

I have so much more to share. Please stay in touch with me. You can do that by visiting me on Facebook at fb.me/ElizabethAshAuthor.

You can also sign up for my email list if you want to be notified when my next book comes out. Visit ElizabethAshAuthor.com and follow the link at the bottom.

With great gratitude for listening, I wish you well on your journey.

www.ingramcontent.com/pod-product-compliance
Lightning Source LLC
Chambersburg PA
CBHW052120070526
44584CB00017B/2571